The Mustangs

by

J. M. Roever & Wilfried Roever

illustrated by

J. M. Roever

Steck-Vaughn Company
An Intext Publisher
Austin, Texas

ISBN 0-8114-7733-9
Library of Congress Catalog Card Number 71-151703

The Mustangs

One of the most colorful chapters in the history of the old Wild West is the story of the mustangs.

In 1846 when Ulysses S. Grant was a lieutenant in the army, he watched mustangs cross a Texas prairie. He reported that the herd spread out as far as the eye could see to the right, and just as far to the left. There were probably one million mustangs in Texas at that time and another million scattered throughout the West.

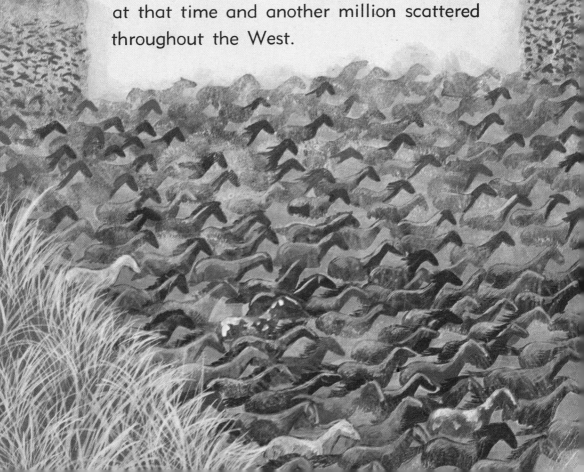

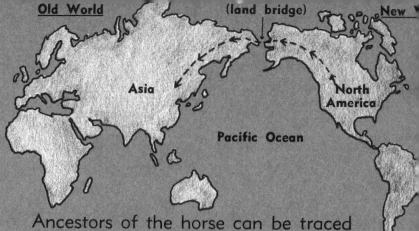

Asia

Pacific Ocean

North America

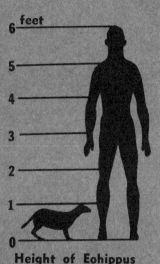

Height of Eohippus

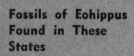

Fossils of Eohippus Found in These States

Ancestors of the horse can be traced far back into prehistoric times. But the horse as we know it today began with Eohippus (ee-o-hip-us) some 58 million years ago. Prehistoric horses developed until Equus (ek-kwus), the modern horse appeared. Fossils of the earliest horse-type animals have been found in North America.

Some ancient horses migrated from North America into Asia. They used the same land bridge by which early man and ancient buffalo crossed into North America. About 10,000 years ago, the wild horse mysteriously disappeared from North and South America. Only in the Old World did Equus survive to be tamed by man.

Eohippus (eo—*dawn*, hippus—*horse*) Lived about 60 Million Years Ago

The Horse Family

There are many kinds of domestic or tame horses. The Przewalski (prez-<u>vahl</u>-ski) horse is the only true wild horse in the world today. The zebra, onager (<u>ahn</u>-eh-jer), and African wild donkey are also members of the wild-horse family.

Onager
(Asia, India,
westward to Palestine)

Wild Donkey
(Africa)

Zebra
(Africa)

Przewalski Horse
(Gobi Desert)

3

The Horse Returns to North America

The first horses to reach the New World were brought by Christopher Columbus. Then in 1519, sixteen horses were taken from Cuba to the mainland of Mexico by Hernando Cortez and his army. The horses carried the Spanish adventurers across Mexico in the search for land and gold.

As the Spaniards conquered and settled the New World, more horses were brought from Spain. Others came from Spanish ranches in the West Indies and Cuba. Many settlers and even church missions raised the beautiful Spanish horses.

The Indians of Mexico had never seen horses. They believed that Spanish soldiers on horseback were four-legged monsters which could come apart. The conquering Spaniards forced the Indians to work at the missions and ranches.

Over the years the Indians watched the Spanish horsemen and realized that horses would obey the commands of their riders. In the darkness of night, many Indians climbed upon the horses and galloped away from their Spanish masters.

The Indian and the Horse

Often the Indians who had taken horses rode back to the ranches and missions and drove off more Spanish horses. Indians on foot traded beads and furs for horses of their own. Soon many Indians rode horseback.

Sometimes an Indian tribe attacked enemy Indian camps and captured their horses. The Indians did not try to train horses born in their own herds. They preferred to obtain trained horses from the Spanish settlers.

In 1680 the Apaches and Navahos joined the Pueblo Indians in their attack on the Spanish settlers in New Mexico. Fleeing Spaniards left behind large herds of horses which the Indians gladly captured. Twelve to fourteen years later, a mighty Spanish army reconquered the Pueblos and drove the remaining Indians out onto the open Plains. For 150 years the Plains Indians ruled the prairies and kept the Spaniards from moving north. They attacked the American settlers as they tried to win the West. The Indians on their horses were known and feared by all.

Mustangs—Horses without Masters

As the history of the West unfolded, thousands of horses moved across the land. Horses were raided and traded, stolen and scattered, lost, stampeded, left behind, and turned loose. Soon new horses began to appear on the western scene. They were the untamed offspring of Spanish horses.

Spaniards called a runaway horse mesteño (mess-ten-yo), meaning "stray." Americans changed the name to mustang. Mustangs were free-roaming fugitives— the wild horses of the West. What a breathtaking sight the mustangs made as they thundered across the prairies! Their flying hooves churned up clouds of dust when they raced through canyons and across mesas. They lived in a world without fences or saddles. The mustangs belonged to the land, and the land belonged to them.

The Era of Mustangs

The American wilderness provided everything that a horse needed—sparkling rivers, abundant grasslands, fresh air, and endless territory.

In 1775 more than 500 Spanish horses were taken to the San Francisco Bay area. The horses were not fenced in, and by 1800 they were running wild. The California mustangs numbered in the thousands.

Most mustangs of the Great Plains were runaway Indian horses that had fled during the excitement and confusion of tribal wars. Some mustangs escaped from battles between Indians and cavalry or broke away during Indian horse raids.

General Sam Houston

Texas

San Jacinto
1836

General Santa Anna

Many herds of Texas mustangs resulted from the war between Texas and Mexico. When General Sam Houston defeated the Mexican army in 1836, Mexican ranchers fled across the Rio Grande. Their abandoned horses soon were racing across the Texas grasslands.

Shortly before the Civil War, mustang herds reached their greatest numbers. Mustangs roamed Texas prairies and raced through coastal valleys in California. They inhabited the Great Plains from Mexico all the way into Canada.

FOAL
(up to one year)

FILLY
(young female horse
up to three years old)

COLT
(young male h
up to three year

MARE
(adult female
horse)

STALLIC
(*stahl-yc*
adult male

The Mustang Family Group

Usually mustangs ran together in bands
of 15 to 20 horses. This mustang family
group was called a manada (ma-nah-dah)
and was led by the smartest mare. Each
manada roamed over an area about 15 miles
wide. Mustangs left their home range
only if food or water became scarce.

When something frightened the small
bands of mustangs, they joined other
manadas and raced across the prairies.
Many horsemen believe that the mustangs
often ran together for the sheer joy of
running, raising dust and being free.

Cougars and wolves sometimes threatened
the young horses.
Usually mustangs could
escape any enemy
by running away.

If an adult horse decided
to fight, it could easily
defeat any predator.

13

The Stallion—Master of the Manada

Each manada was ruled by a stallion.
Only the strongest, smartest, swiftest
stallions were able to control manadas.
Young stallions often tried to steal
mares from another stallion's family.
Then a terrible fight took place.

The battling warriors struck each other
with their hooves and bit one another
with their long, sharp teeth. Angry
screams filled the air. The defeated
stallion fled from his angry conqueror,
and the victorious stallion
rounded up his band.

This rare pinto stallion is marked with a dark "shield" over its ears, head, neck, and chest. The Plains Indians believed such a horse had magical powers.

The lordly stallion fiercely guarded his manada. He usually stood on a small hilltop near his band. There he could watch for danger as he grazed. He would not allow his band to approach its drinking place until he had tested the water. If an enemy approached, the stallion put his manada to flight. The mustangs followed the lead mare, while the stallion ran alongside or circled behind the band and forced the slower horses to run faster. Master stallions were seldom caught or tamed by man.

Some Colors of Mustangs

CHESTNUT

Star

Stripe (nose)

BAY

APPALOOSA

Sock

Stocking

PINTO OR PAINT

Blaze

PALOMINO

Stripe (leg)

Stripe (back)

BLACK

GRAY

DUN

Anatomy of a Mustang

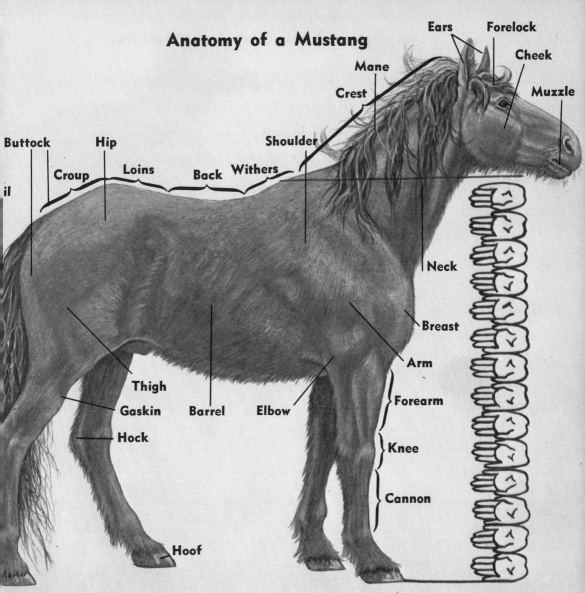

Ears · Forelock · Cheek · Mane · Crest · Muzzle · Buttock · Hip · Loins · Shoulder · Croup · Back · Withers · il · Neck · Breast · Arm · Thigh · Forearm · Gaskin · Barrel · Elbow · Knee · Hock · Cannon · Hoof

The height of a horse is measured in hands all over the world. One hand is 4 inches. This sorrel-colored mustang is 14 hands and 1 inch tall at the withers.

17

Appearance and Senses of Mustangs

Most mustangs differed in appearance from their tame Spanish ancestors. They often had large heads, long ears, and small bodies. The hair of mustangs grew long and thick to protect them from harsh weather. Sometimes their tails were tangled with cockleburs. Jughead, bronco, fuzztail, and broomtail were names given to the rough-looking mustangs.

A keen sense of smell warned mustangs of approaching danger. They also had excellent eyesight and hearing.

Legendary Stallions

Occasionally, a mustang was born more beautiful than any Spanish horse. With proud neck and flowing mane, he caught the eye of all who saw him.

Many legends revolved around beautiful mustang stallions. One of the most famous was the Ghost Horse of the Prairies or the Pacing White Stallion. Indian legends tell of Black Devil, who attacked and killed any man who tried to capture him. Blue Streak and Starface were pursued for many years. Folktales say these magnificent stallions raced off the edges of cliffs and chose death rather than the saddles and fences of humans.

19

ck Devil

**The Pacing White Stallion—
Ghost Horse of the Prairies**

Mustangs and Men

When mustangs began to gather in herds, many men tried to capture them. Some Indians lassoed their mustangs after an exciting chase on horseback. The adventurers who caught wild horses were called "mustangers." The easiest and safest way to obtain mustangs was to catch foals. Mustangers chased mares who had foals until the young ones grew tired. Then, the foals were caught and raised with tame horses.

Some brave, young mustangers would ride their own horses side by side with a galloping mustang. Suddenly, the mustanger would leap from his tame horse onto the racing, wild one. A looped rope was thrown over the mustang's head and around its nose. The daring rider stayed on the horse's back until it grew tired. Then, using the nose rope, the mustanger guided the captive horse to its new home.

Often entire herds of mustangs were
trapped when they were chased into hidden
corrals or canyons and the entrances
closed behind them. Then, each horse was
roped and broken for market. Sometimes
mustangers would follow a manada for
days and not give the wild horses any
time to eat or drink or sleep. One by one
the weary mustangs were roped. Only the
swiftest and strongest horses escaped.

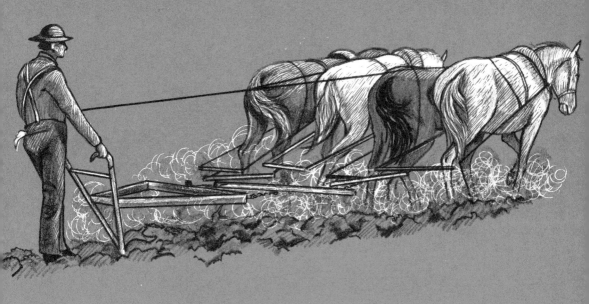

The Return to Saddles and Fences

So it was that countless mustangs were forced to return to the domestic life of their Spanish ancestors. Life in the wilderness had made these mustangs very strong and fast. They could endure many hardships. Mustangs were perfect horses to help build America.

Captured mustangs were driven east to the Mississippi River and sold to plantations where they hauled heavy cotton wagons. Other mustangs were sold to settlers to pull their plows.

California mustangs were used for the famous Pony Express, and Texas Rangers often rode captured wild horses. Mustang cow ponies helped control great herds of Longhorn cattle. Rodeos and Wild West shows purchased bad-tempered mustangs as bucking broncos. Outlaws and lawmen, Indians and cavalry, frontiersmen, cowboys, buffalo hunters, gamblers, traders, prospectors, surveyors, trappers, and ranchers found adventure, wealth, or misfortune while riding captured mustangs.

Wild and Unwanted

As years passed, ranchers grew angry with the wild mustangs. Stallions stole valuable mares away from the ranches. Mustangs broke down fences and drove cattle away from water. They ate grass needed for livestock. Soon hunters were hired to destroy the mustangs.

Although the wild horses had often slipped away from men, lassos, and hidden fences, they could not escape from guns. The herd of mustangs rapidly disappeared.

A Natural History Map of the Mustangs

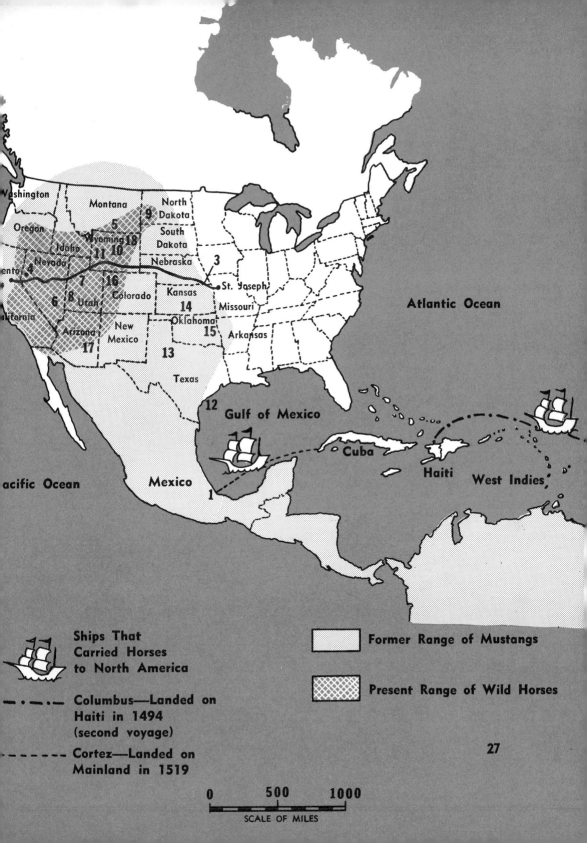

Washington

Montana

North Dakota

Oregon

5

9

Idaho

Wyoming 18

South Dakota

11 10

Nevada

Nebraska

ento

4

7

16

3

St. Joseph

8

Utah

Colorado

Kansas

6

Missouri

14

lifornia

Arizona

New Mexico

Oklahoma

15

Arkansas

17

13

Atlantic Ocean

Texas

12

Gulf of Mexico

Cuba

acific Ocean

Mexico

Haiti

West Indies

1

Ships That Carried Horses to North America

—·—·— **Columbus—Landed on Haiti in 1494 (second voyage)**

— — — **Cortez—Landed on Mainland in 1519**

[ ] **Former Range of Mustangs**

[▨] **Present Range of Wild Horses**

27

0   500   1000

SCALE OF MILES

Annie and the Airplanes

Airplanes brought a new danger to the remaining mustang herds. Wild horses chased by airplanes quickly grew weak and tired. Between 1945 and 1959 men ruthlessly hunted mustangs with airplanes. Then the horses were shipped in trucks to pet food canneries.

In 1950 Velma B. Johnson saw a truckload of captured mustangs near Reno, Nevada. Outraged and saddened, Mrs. Johnson began a tireless crusade to save the wild horses. Soon people nicknamed her "Wild Horse Annie."

Velma Johnson, "Wild Horse Annie," and Her Mustang *Hobo*

In 1959 Mrs. Johnson spoke to Congress about the sad fate of our wild horses. That year a law was passed to protect the horses from hunters in motorized vehicles. Refuges for wild horses were created in a number of western states.

But wild horses were still persecuted, and in 1971 congressmen designed a bill to protect wild horses as part of our national heritage—living symbols of pioneer spirit and freedom. Once men needed mustangs to survive in the Old West, but wild horses must have the help of men to survive in the space age.

Letters from Horse Lovers, Conservationists, and School Children

Save Our Horses

To Congress

Yes— Protection

The Capitol in Washington, D.C.

No Protection

Pet Foo

Wild Horse— Symbol of Our National Heritage

29

Never again will the hooves of two million racing mustangs thunder across the grasslands of America. But they have left their imprint on the geography of our land. Mustang Island, Wild Horse Prairie, Wild Horse Creek, Wild Horse Mountain, Wild Horse Plain, Wild Horse Canyon, Spotted Horse Creek—these colorfully named places remind us of the wild and free horses of the Old West. Perhaps, if you close your eyes, you can still see them—galloping, galloping, galloping across the pages of history.